EARTH

OUR PLANET IN SPACE

EARTH

OUR PLANET IN SPACE

SEYMOUR SIMON

FOUR WINDS PRESS
NEW YORK

PICTURE CREDITS

The author wishes to acknowledge for the use of photographs and diagrams:

NASA: Frontispiece, 7, 9, 10, 11, 12, 13, 15, 16, 22, 23, 24, 25, 26, 28, 29, 30, 31, 32

Yerkes Observatory Photograph, University of Chicago: 14, 18, 20, 21

Soil Conservation Service, USDA: 19

10 9 8 7 6 5 4 3 2 1

The text of this book is set in 18 pt. Garamond.
The illustrations are black-and-white photographs.

Library of Congress Cataloging in Publication Data
Simon, Seymour.
Earth, our planet in space.
Summary: A basic introduction to the Solar System
and Earth's place in it, seasons, and Earth's topography.
1. Earth—Juvenile literature. 2. Earth—
Photographs from space—Juvenile literature.
[1. Earth] I. Title.
QB631.S56 1984 525 83-11706
ISBN 0-590-07884-4

To my niece and nephews,

Ellen, Stephen, Jonathan, and Richard

You live on Earth. You may live in a city or in the country. You may live where snow often falls or where it never snows at all. But wherever you call home, you live on Earth. We all live on Earth.

Earth is in space. Space is outside the layer of air that surrounds Earth. Here is how Earth looks from miles and miles out in space. The dark places are seas, and the gray places are lands. Some of the seas and lands are covered by white clouds. The large white spot at the bottom is the snow-covered land of Antarctica.

Earth is a planet. A planet is a large world that travels around the sun.

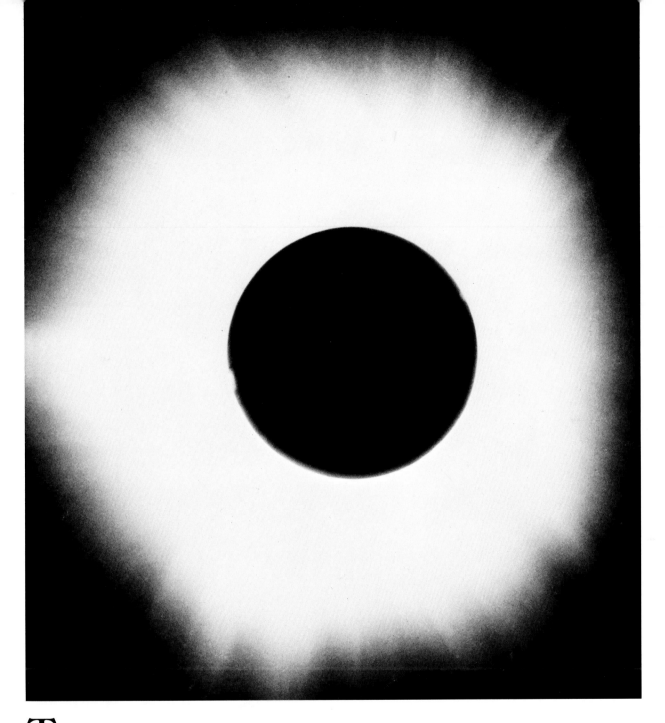

The sun is not a planet. It's a star
a million times bigger than Earth.
Light and heat come from the sun.

Earth is not the only planet that travels around the sun. Nine planets travel around the sun. Some of the planets are bigger than Earth, and some are smaller. Together, the sun and the planets are called the Solar System.

Here is a picture of part of the Solar System. Eight photographs were used to make this picture. Earth is shown rising over the surface of the moon. The sun is shown peeking out from behind Earth. Just to the left of Earth is the planet Venus. From the left, the other planets shown are Jupiter, Mercury, Mars, and Saturn. The planets not shown are Uranus, Neptune, and Pluto.

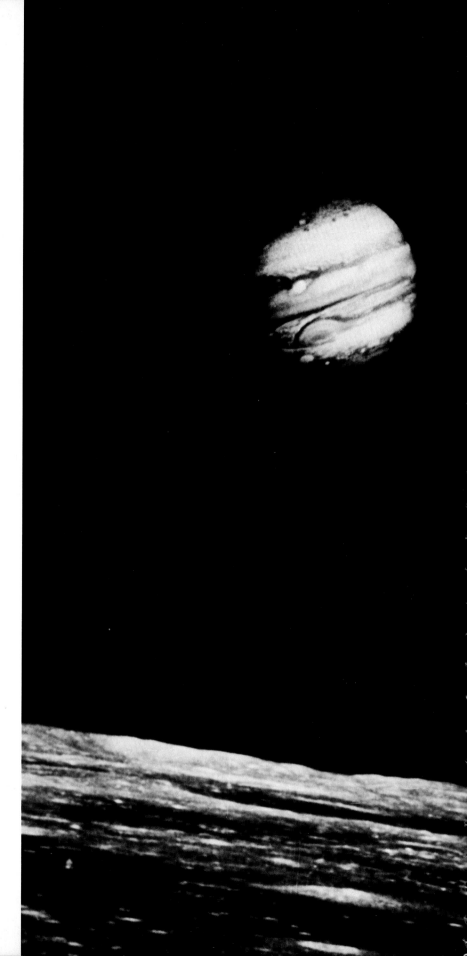

In this photograph Earth's shadow is traveling across the moon. Many years ago, people thought that Earth was flat, but you can see that the shadow of Earth is a curve. The shadow helped people learn that Earth is round. Today, scientists photograph and measure Earth from spaceships. They say that our planet is shaped almost like a ball. It is very slightly pear-shaped.

In the photograph on the right you can see how Earth looks from the surface of the moon. Light from the sun falls on one half of Earth at a time. One half of Earth is light while the other half is dark. From the moon you can see the light side but not the dark side of Earth.

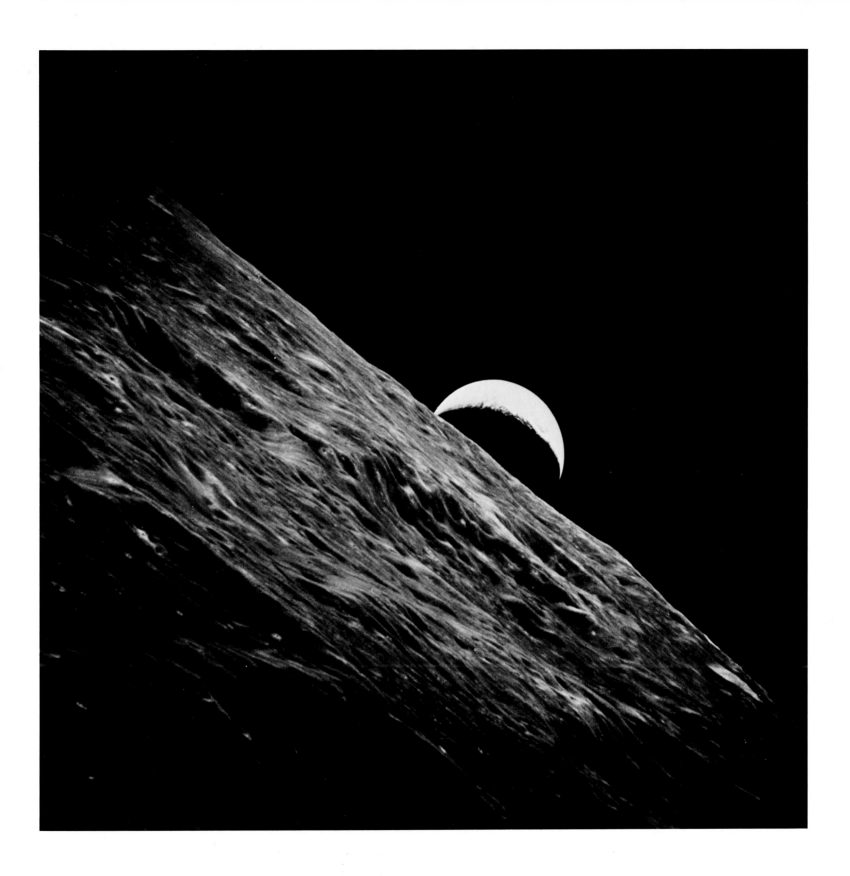

Earth is spinning all the time. It spins like a giant top. If you lived on the light side it would be daytime. If you lived on the dark side it would be nighttime.

The light side spins away from the sun. To a person living on the light side, it looks as if the sun is going down. But the sun is not moving. It is Earth that is spinning. It takes one day, or twenty-four hours, for Earth to spin around once.

The dark side spins toward the sun. To a person living on the dark side, it looks as if the sun is rising. Day comes to the side of Earth that has been in darkness.

While Earth is spinning, it also travels around the sun in a path called an orbit. It takes Earth one year, or about 365 days, to travel around the sun once.

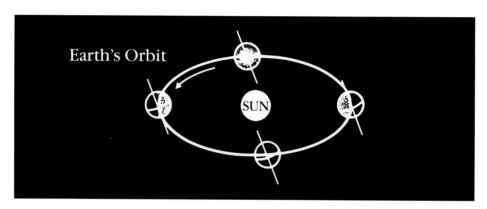

Earth is about 93 million miles from the sun. If the sun were closer, Earth would broil. If the sun were farther, Earth would freeze. The sun is at just the right distance for the living things on Earth.

There is no other planet that is the same distance from our sun, so there is no planet that has the same temperatures as Earth. As far as we know, Earth is the only one of the planets that has plants, animals, and people.

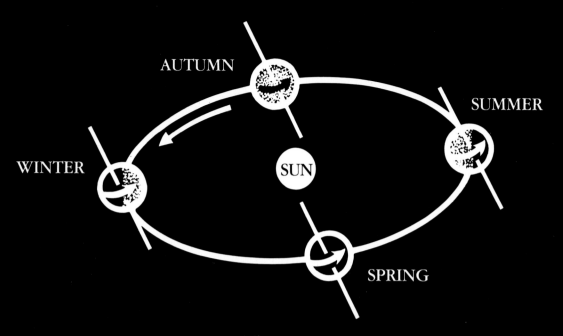

AUTUMN

SUMMER

WINTER

SUN

SPRING

The Seasons

One half of Earth has winter while the other half has summer. When Earth travels around the sun, it is tilted a little to one side. For part of the year, the northern half of Earth is tilted toward the sun. When this happens, the northern half of Earth has summer.

At that time the southern half of Earth is tilted away from the sun, so southern places have winter.

The seasons change. Winter follows summer, and summer follows winter. As Earth travels around the sun, the north is tilted away. The northern places become colder. The southern half of Earth is tilted toward the sun, and summer comes. As the year goes by, the place where you live on Earth warms up or cools off.

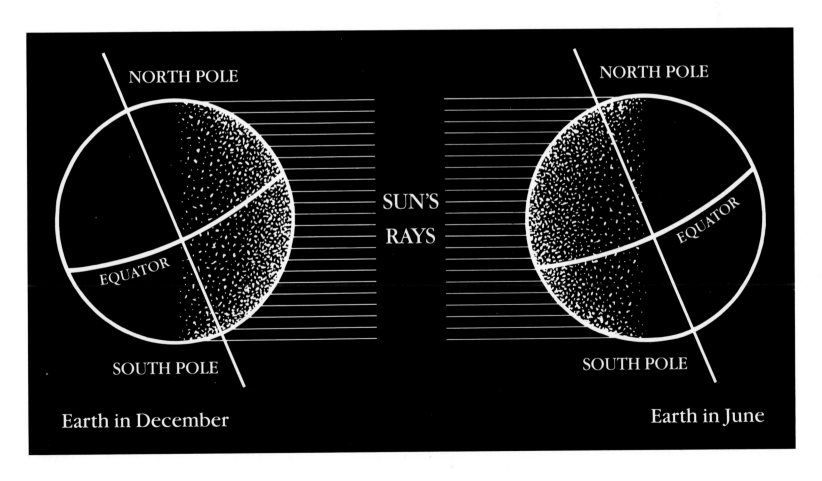

NORTH POLE

EQUATOR

SOUTH POLE

SUN'S
RAYS

NORTH POLE

EQUATOR

SOUTH POLE

Earth in December

Earth in June

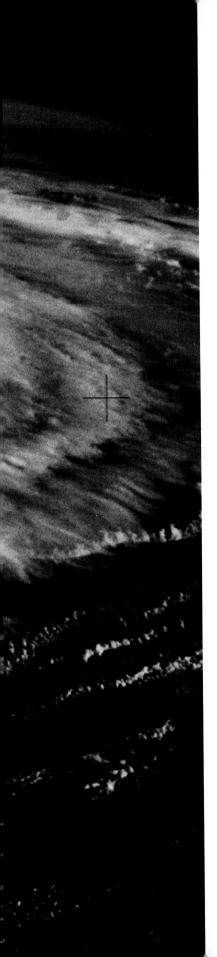

Earth has a blanket of air around it that keeps it from getting too hot or too cold. The blanket of air is called the atmosphere. Earth's atmosphere is made of gases and bits of dust and water. The atmosphere helps make Earth a planet full of living things. No other planet has an atmosphere like Earth's.

Earth is like a giant magnet. The space around a magnet is called a magnetic field. Earth's magnetic field acts like a shield. It helps protect living things from dangerous radiation from the sun that can kill everything on Earth.

The magnetic field sometimes makes colored lights that you can see in the night sky. These lights are called an aurora. Here is a photograph of an aurora.

The surface of planet Earth is covered with land and water. This is a photograph of lower California. The dark places are seas, the lighter places are lands, and the white clouds are part of the air.

There is much more water than land on the surface of our planet. Oceans cover nearly three-quarters of Earth.

The lands on Earth's surface are always changing. Here is a photograph of the highest mountains on Earth—the Himalayas in Asia. Mountains are pushed up by changes inside our planet. The Himalayas are still rising. The snow-covered mountains on the left are over twelve thousand feet high. The dark line is a deep river valley. Over many years the river has scraped deep into the land.

The surface of the land wears away. Here is a photograph of Niagara Falls. The waterfalls in the middle of the photo are about three thousand feet wide and nearly two hundred feet high. Over the years the water of the Falls has worn away, or eroded, the rock underneath. The Falls have moved six miles farther upriver in the last few thousand years.

In the winter, water freezes and becomes ice or snow. The ice breaks up rock and wears it away. Snow piles up and pushes down on the land. In this photograph you can see how snow and ice have worked to change the surface of the land.

People also change the surface of the land. They farm the land. They dig into the land and use the rocks and minerals they find. This is a photograph of Phoenix, Arizona. Can you see the ways the land has been changed?

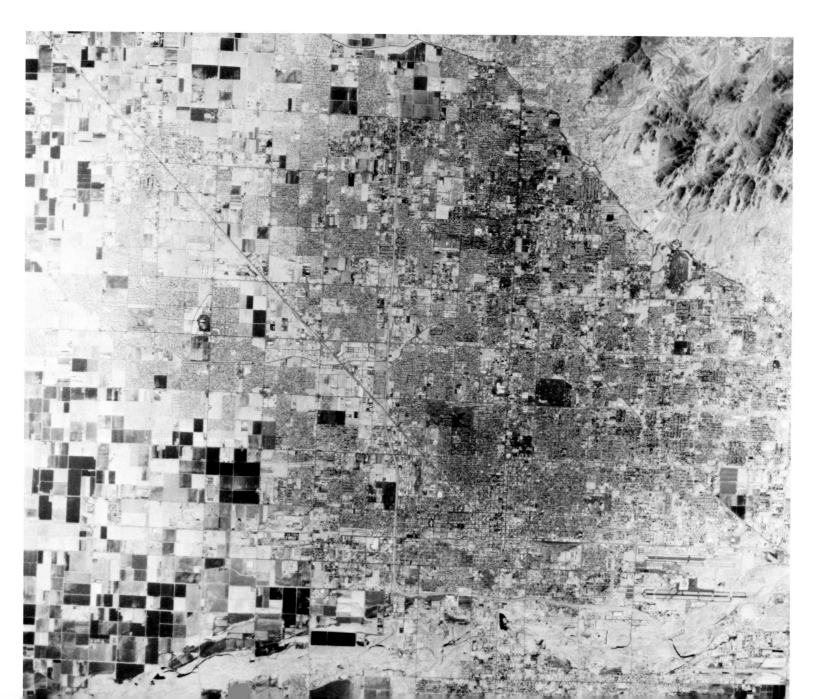

This is New York City. Millions of people live here in thousands of buildings. Yet this great city is just a tiny speck on Earth's surface. To an astronaut on the moon, which is Earth's closest neighbor in space, no signs of people can be seen.

People have always dreamed of leaving Earth to explore other worlds in space. We have already landed on the moon. We have sent spaceships to explore the other planets in our Solar System. We have learned much about these planets and about Earth, too. Earth and the other planets were formed at the same time and in the same way. Clues to Earth's history can be found out in space.